AVOIDING PLAGIARISM

AVOIDING PLAGIARISM

Write Better Papers in APA, Chicago, and Harvard Citation Styles

DR. KEN K. WONG

U21GLOBAL | UNIVERSITY OF TORONTO

iUniverse, Inc.
Bloomington

Avoiding Plagiarism
Write Better Papers in APA, Chicago, and Harvard Citation Styles

iUniverse books may be ordered through booksellers or by contacting:

iUniverse
1663 Liberty Drive
Bloomington, IN 47403
www.iuniverse.com
1-800-Authors (1-800-288-4677)

Because of the dynamic nature of the Internet, any Web addresses or links contained in this book may have changed since publication and may no longer be valid. The views expressed in this work are solely those of the author and do not necessarily reflect the views of the publisher, and the publisher hereby disclaims any responsibility for them.

Any people depicted in stock imagery provided by Thinkstock are models, and such images are being used for illustrative purposes only.

Certain stock imagery © Thinkstock.

ISBN: 978-1-4502-7628-3 (pbk)
ISBN: 978-1-4502-7629-0 (cloth)
ISBN: 978-1-4502-7630-6 (ebk)

Printed in the United States of America

iUniverse rev. date: 12/27/2010

To my wife Winnie, and my family members
Hello Ma, Hello Dad, and Hello Chiu

Thank you for your love, understanding, patience, and confidence.

ABOUT THE AUTHOR

Dr. Ken Kwong-Kay Wong

Dr. Ken K. Wong is a U21Global Marketing Professor and Subject Area Coordinator, training corporate executives and MBA students from over 70 countries. In 2008 and 2009, he received the Faculty Excellence Award, and was honoured in all three award categories, including: Outstanding Professor, Most Innovative Professor and Excellence in Online Education. Since 2003, Dr. Wong has been developing and lecturing marketing courses at the University of Toronto's School of Continuing Studies and also at various institutions of higher education in North America.

Dr. Wong's research interests include marketing for luxury brands, customer relationship management and online education. His articles have appeared in peer-reviewed international journals such as *Telecommunications Policy, Service Industries Journal*, and *Journal of Database Marketing and Customer Strategy Management*. Dr. Wong is also the author of the SCS lecture series in the areas of International Marketing, Advertising, PR & Publicity, E-Business, and Retail Merchandising. His latest work includes *Approved Marketing Plans for New Products and Services, CRM in Action, Putting a Stake in the Ground, and Discovering Marketing in 38 Hours.*

Prior to entering the academic field, Dr. Wong was the Vice President of Marketing at TeraGo Networks (TSX: TGO) and had previously served as Director of eProduct Marketing at the e-commerce division of PSINet (NASDAQ: PSIX). He had also carried progressive product marketing roles at Sprint Canada and TELUS Mobility.

Certified by the American Marketing Association as a Professional Certified Marketer, Dr. Wong completed his Bachelor of Science degree at the University of Toronto and holds the International MBA degree from Nyenrode Business Universiteit in the Netherlands. He earned his Doctor of Business Administration degree from the University of Newcastle, Australia and has completed executive education programmes at both Kellogg and Queen's.

CONTENTS

Chapter 8 – Harvard Style   66

Foreword

One of the biggest challenges facing education today is intellectual integrity. When I went to school in the 70s, much of the work I created was painstakingly written by hand. Fast-forward to today and it is rare to see anything written by hand at all. In the modern era, documents are electronic and students have access to unlimited amounts of information at their fingertips through the Web. The impact that technology has had, and will continue to have, on education is enormous.

While the broadening of access to rich information resources might be considered as advancement in education, it also has its downsides. When one has access to so much information, is one tempted to simply search for a solution rather than actively think about creating one? Or to frame it another way, is thinking reduced from an inventive process to a manufacturing process involving the composition of prefabricated ideas? The naysayers amongst us may argue that technology, or rather the wealth of information afforded by the technology, blunts creatively. In short, the more we Google, the more we lessen our capacity to think independently. On the other hand, others might argue that technology is a tool that enriches our thinking by allowing us to connect existing ideas and build upon them further.

Regardless of whether we agree with the positive or negative view, technology is here to stay and the signs are that it will become even more fused into education and our lives in general. This means that academic institutions, more than ever, need to deal with the pressing issue of plagiarism which returns me to my point about intellectual integrity. The digitization of information has made it effortless to cut-and-paste from one document to another. Left unchecked, a cut-and-paste culture allows students to present collages of work that may be devoid of any personal intellectual fabric. Students will be tempted to surf superficially for a solution rather than immerse themselves in deep thinking. This clearly is intellectual stagnation, not advancement.

Academic institutions therefore play an important role in educating students in the difference between blatant "cut and paste" and the careful integration of other people's work in one's own work. To the ignorant, there may be no difference at all. However, proper referencing and citation is an essential skill that needs to be taught and practiced. This book by Dr. Ken Wong is therefore timely. Unlike other resources in this area, it provides additional information on tools for similarity detection and citation generation. Educators in particular will find this book a valuable resource.

Professor Wing Lam
Dean, U21Global Graduate School

Preface

The idea of writing a book on citing and referencing styles seems to be a crazy one. An endless stream of information is available online, and students need just a few seconds to "Google" the information they seek. Unfortunately, the official web sites of APA (American Psychological Association) and Chicago Press display limited examples that are adequate for graduate-level writing. To make the situation worse, some students rely on unverified materials from web sites that lack credibility, or download outdated writing guides that are published by universities from other continents. It becomes a problem because these writing guidelines and examples are not consistent. Furthermore, they often do not cover the latest citation styles driven by the latest technology development. Questions like "Which style should I follow?" and "How do I cite a YouTube video?" keep flooding my e-mail box.

The official writing guides published by American Psychological Association and the University of Chicago Press, are materials that virtually none of my students are willing to invest in. The relatively heavy weight and high costs of these masterpieces have put off some of my students. In my opinion, asking students to buy these great books for studying is like pulling teeth. The fact is that students in MBA-level courses are still challenged in their academic writing. The challenges they encounter include:

1. Having no idea why proper citing and referencing is required.
2. Not being able to choose the correct writing style for their papers.
3. Being incapable of using proper citing and referencing styles in their assignments.

Poorly written work not only merits poor academic marks; in extreme cases, the student commits a serious academic offense in the form of plagiarism. Hence, it is vital for students to learn proper writing and referencing styles especially in the early stage of their graduate study.

Although many of my students have reviewed the materials

presented in this book, I know that it is not perfect and in fact, it is far from perfect. While this book may not be a replacement of your official APA and Chicago handbooks, I believe that the content serves you well in helping you avoid mark deduction due to improper citing and referencing. As a writer, I would like to hear your feedback about my little book. Your suggestions will be of great help in shaping the future edition of this book so feel free to drop me an e-mail.

Dr. Ken K. Wong　黃廣基 博士

Ottawa, Ontario, Canada
December 3, 2010

e-mail: ken.wong@utoronto.ca
e-mail: kwong@u21global.edu.sg
Twitter: http://twitter.com/drkenkwong
Web: http://www.introductiontomarketing.ca/

ACKNOWLEDGEMENT

In completing my book, I have drawn support from many people and thus feel a huge debt of gratitude. I would like to thank the International Editorial Board for providing me with valuable input and constructive criticism to my work.

International Editorial Board:

Abdalla Gholoum
Annie Nyet Ngo Chan
Basil Pathrose
Chee Wai Hoo
Dutta Bholanath
Ekaterina Leonova
Engelbert Atangana
LH Kho
Khurshid Jussawalla
Kishore Pai
Lothar R. Pehl
Narendra Nesarikar
Rajen Kumar Shah
Richard Anthony
Shama Dewji
Tasneem Tailor
Vicky Yan Xu
Vien Cortes
Zulfikar Jiffry

Chapter 1 –
Introduction

"When in Rome, do as the Romans do." (St. Ambrose, 387 A.D.)

Academic writing is different from your day-to-day business report or blog writing. There are certain rules that you must follow or else your professor will deduct marks from your work. Furthermore, academic journals require authors to follow a particular writing style for their manuscript submissions. Unfortunately, most university students are not being taught this subject during their undergraduate studies. As a result, I am dedicating this book to help you master the art of academic writing.

First, know that there are different kinds of citing and referencing styles. In the field of business, the common ones are APA, Chicago and Harvard citation styles. I will cover each of them with examples later in this book. How about MLA, Oxford (documentary-note), and Vancouver (URM)? I am not going to talk about the MLA and Oxford styles because they are only common in Humanities courses such as history, philosophy, language and arts. I am also not going to spend time on the Vancouver style because it is mostly used in the biomedical field. If you absolutely want to learn about these citation styles, please visit the following web sites:

- **MLA**: Modern Language Association (www.mla.org)

- **Oxford**: http://www.deakin.edu.au/current-students/study-support/study-skills/handouts/oxford-docnote.php

- **Vancouver**: International Committee of Medical Journal Editors (www.icmje.org)

In the next chapter, I will discuss the issue of plagiarism and give you some tips to avoid the problem. Then, the concepts of in-text citations and referencing will be introduced to you in great detail. In chapter 5, I will show you some online citation tool and software that you can use for academic writing. Finally, selected citation and referencing examples using APA, Chicago and Harvard styles are presented.

Chapter 2 –
Strategies for Avoiding Plagiarism

What is Plagiarism?

Plagiarism refers to the use of others' ideas and presenting them as your own. It is intellectual theft and is considered a serious academic offence. The most common type of plagiarism is a direct "Copy and Paste" action. For instance, copying the content from a book and making a book of a similar title, is definitely an act of plagiarism. But how about copying just a sentence or two? Well, if you cite my sentences properly using a quotation format, there should be no problem.

The smart students will put up their hands and ask, "Dr. Wong, what if I paraphrase your sentence?" In my opinion, this is still reverse engineering because you are taking another's thoughts as your own. Remember, your professor is interested in seeing your critical thinking skills so instead of paraphrasing others' points, why don't you critique their thoughts and add in your own analysis? The brave students would even ask me questions like "Dr. Wong, how many words can I copy directly without being caught by those anti-plagiarism software?" My answer: 5 words.

While some students intentionally plagiarize others' work to cheat, I believe that there are many students out there who commit plagiarism and related academic offences unintentionally; that is, they commit plagiarism simply because they do not know how to write properly. Common mistakes include:

1. **Incorrect in-text citations and references:** the publication year is wrong and the author's name is misspelled.

2. **Incomplete in-text citations and references:** this often happens in a long paragraph where multiple thoughts from different authors are mentioned.

3. **Lack of reference:** student forgets to provide the corresponding reference after including the in-text citation.

4. **Assemblage:** student spends too much time in making reference to others' thoughts (although with proper citing/referencing) and makes little original contribution.

5. **Self-plagiarism:** students recycle their own papers that were previously submitted in other classes.

What you need to remember is that professors have tools to spot out plagiarism not only in paper assignments, but also in discussion board contributions. Your work will be compared to millions of web pages and homework database among most universities in just a matter of seconds, so do not risk committing plagiarism!

The Problem of Ctrl-C & Ctrl-V

The plagiarism issue is a difficult topic to discuss with students. This is because some students, especially those who come from certain countries where their educational system is not that well developed, have never been taught about this issue in school. In some cases, students have heard about it but because they have never seen any actual enforcement of the school policy (e.g. student dismissal), they believe that "Plagiarism is not a problem until I get caught!". Students go ahead and plagiarize without realizing the seriousness of such academic offence.

In 2010, I posted a blog entry at the education section of the Asian Correspondent web site to discuss the issue of plagiarism. Many students have found my article useful so let me share it with you:

> Plagiarism is a serious academic offence. The problem is getting bigger and bigger as students can now "extract" information to re-use in their assignments in a matter of seconds. The smart ones

know that you're using tools like Turnitin to catch them so they turn to Synonymizer software to do better reverse engineering. To get the students understand the issue of practicing Ctrl-C & Ctrl-V better, I recently acted as a story teller and my MBA students seem to get the message pretty good. Feel free to spread the story if you find it useful:

John and Mary enrolled into a cooking class in a prestigious culinary school. After learning all of those fancy cooking techniques for three months, it's time to show off their cooking skills during a tasting event which is also their final examination. They were given the whole afternoon to prepare for their meals at home and bring back their 'creation' to school during dinner time. The judges were eager to taste their delicious dishes.

Some unexpected situations happened at noon. The power went out in the dorm where both John and Mary were staying. So, the electric cooker, stove and fridge were not working. John, being very nervous, went out to several upscale restaurants nearby to order some takeouts. Mary, who's also getting very nervous, went out to shop at a nearby supermarket.

At the evening tasting event, John happily put his five-course meal on the table for the judges to taste. Mary, on the other hand, took out a loaf of bread and spent 10 minutes to make her "Club Sandwich" using some pre-packaged deli, tomato, lettuce and mayonnaise in front of the judges.

The result? John got a failing grade while Mary got a 82 percent.

Do you know why?

P.S.: If your students are using Macs, replace "Control-C and Control-V" with "Command-C and Command-V".

By Dr Ken Wong

The original blog entry and response to my article can be found at: http://asiancorrespondent.com/U21Global/the-problem-of-ctrl-c-&-ctrl-v

USING THE TURNITIN ONLINE CHECKING TOOL

Without doubt, Turnitin.com is one of the most popular online plagiarism checking tools that is used by universities and colleges around the world. While Turnitin is often used by professors, many schools have actually purchased campus-wide license to allow students to check papers on their own. Please ask your professor to learn if you can utilize this online tool during your study.

The process of checking papers via Turnitin is very simple. Once you've logged in with your username and password, all you need to do is to select your course ID and upload your paper for checking. If your professor has not set up a specific course ID, you can also use the "Quick Submit" function to do a one-time checking of your paper.

Since Turnitin has to check your work against its complex database, it usually takes 3 to 5 minutes to check a paper. The result is presented graphically with a "Similarity Index":

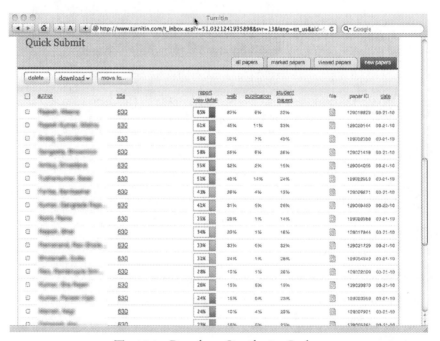

Turnitin Results - Similarity Index

The example here shows all papers that have been examined by the Turnitin system in my class. As you can see from this diagram, most papers have green and yellow color. When the Similarity Index has reached over 50%, the indicator color changes to orange and the most problematic one will be shown in red. For each checking, a detailed examination report is also generated to show you how your paper is being compared to others.

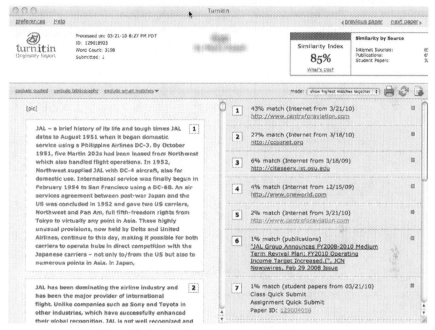

Detailed paper comparison in Turnitin

FREE ONLINE PLAGIARISM CHECKING TOOL

If you do not have access to Turnitin, there is a free tool that you can use over the web. The Plagiarism Checker is an online tool created by Biran Klug of the University of Maryland back in 2002. It is still one of the popular free online tools for checking plagiarism.

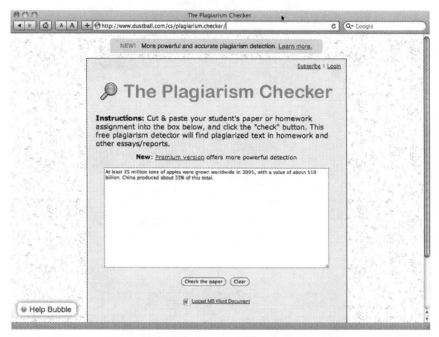

The Plagiarism Checker

You can either paste sentences there for checking, or upload a single MSWord file for checking as well. After pressing the "Check the paper" button, the result is shown almost immediately.

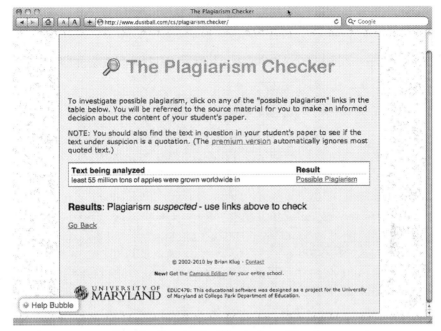

Results from The Plagiarism Checker

This web tool is accessible at:
http://www.dustball.com/cs/plagiarism.checker/

TACKLING DISCUSSION BOARD AND ASSIGNMENT QUESTION

Nobody (myself included) is born an academic writer. It takes time to learn the proper way to research and write about a topic. When I come across cases of plagiarism, I talk to the students and try to understand why the plagiarism occurred. I have found that many students, especially the younger ones in their early 20s, have been so used to taking short-cuts in compiling their papers or discussion board postings.

Here is what they usually do. Let us assume that the topic of interest is about the "Hybrid Car".

Step 1: Google "Hybrid Car" from the web.

Step 2: Copy and paste a large chunk of text into MSWord.

Step 3: Go to Wikipedia and search "Hybrid Car".

Step 4: Copy and paste a large chunk of text into MSWord.

Step 5: Search "Hybrid Car" from those free-essay sites

Step 6: Copy and paste a large chunk of text into MSWord.

Step 7: Move the paragraphs around.

Step 8: Do a "find and replace" in MSWord to change the text to make it fit with the question (e.g. from Green Car to Hybrid Car)

Step 9: Write the introduction and conclusion parts, hoping that the professor will not read through the whole document.

Do you do the same in doing research? If yes, now is the time to change your style and start learning the proper way of writing research papers. I have asked some of my students to use the following procedures, and I have seen substantial improvement in their outputs. Perhaps you can also give it a try!

Step 1: Before doing any googling, spend at least 5 minutes to think why the professor is asking for this topic. Yes, it is about Hybrid Cars but why is it important to know about this kind of cars right now? Is it about pollution? Is it about energy savings? Or is it about international business? What is the key theme of the paper that you are going to write?

Step 2: Let us say that the theme is about pollution, do a research on this topic on the Internet.

Step 3: During your research, see how the launch of the hybrid car is related to pollution. Who are the players in the sectors (e.g. Honda, Toyota, GM..etc)? How are they performing? Who are the customers? What makes consumers choose a Hybrid Car over a traditional gasoline-based vehicle?

Step 4: Write down your findings on a piece of paper in bullet points.

Step 5: Write down the web site address for the relevant pages that you have visited. You will need them for your reference list.

Step 6: Using the bullet points that you have just written on a piece of paper, start writing your paper from scratch in your word processor.

Step 7: Prior to submission, double check whether you have the proper introduction, problem statement, situational overview, analysis and conclusion.

Step 8: Check the visual presentation: Have you made good use of tables and charts to present some of your ideas? How about fixing the fonts and spacing?

Step 9: Spell-check your document and then double-check the in-text citations and references to ensure accuracy.

Chapter 3 –
What are In-text Citations?

When we talk about academic writing, there are two major areas of concern: citations and references. So, what exactly is a "citation"? Also known as "in-text citing", it refers to how you should acknowledge the source of information when you write an article. Let us take a look at the following example:

> In some cases, product lines have had defective rates of greater than 25% (Smith and Susan, 2010).

Here, you are telling your readers that according to researchers John Smith and Mary Susan who published their research findings in 2010, the product lines have had defective rates of greater than 25%. It is important for you to acknowledge the source of information lest the readers think that you conducted the research yourself. Furthermore, your readers may want to know why it is 25% and how this observation is made. By citing the source, your readers can look up the corresponding research article in your reference list to learn more. Citation also gives proper credits to the researchers.

I flip open the May 2009 issue of the Journal of Marketing and find this good example of citation on page 36:

> Prior research has shown that a lenient product return policy potentially creates a competitive advantage for the retailer or manufacturer (Padmanabhan and Png 1997) and increases a customer's likelihood to purchase a product in the first place

(Chu, Gerstner, and Hess 1998; Nasr-Bechwati and Siegal 2005). However, a lenient product return policy is not always ideal (Wood 2001), because it can lead to more product returns (David, Hagerty, and Gerstner 1998) and to "abuse," which can cost the firm more than it benefits (Rust, Zahorik, and Keiningham 1996).

To some, the above paragraph may look a little bit strange and very difficult to read. However, it is a well-written piece academically speaking because it includes proper citations. In my opinion, it is better to over-cite than under-cite because you would not want to commit plagiarism (i.e. presenting others' idea as your own). Of course, you only cite relevant sources so do not list more than five or six papers per citation unless all of them are relevant and influential. If the information is a fact, such as "the sun rises from the East" or "Sushi is a Japanese dish", then you do not need to cite this public knowledge.

In addition to citing reference details at the end of a sentence, you can also consider the following sentence structures:

- As Smith (2010) has pointed out, the...
- According to Smith (2010), this...
- Smith (2010) argues/outlines/states/suggests that...
- In a study in 2010, Smith showed/illustrated that...

If the article that you are referring to is written by several authors, you will see the word "et al." being used starting from the second citation of such article. The first citation will always show the last name of all of the authors. For example, let us say an article is written by four researchers named John Smith, Mary Susan, Peter Lee, and Tommy Kim. If John is the primary author, the first citation will be (Smith, Susan, Lee, & Kim, 2010) and then (Smith et al., 2010) will be used in subsequent citations of this article in your paper.

How About Quotes?

Some students like to use quotations very often. In some problematic cases, they just copy and paste a large chunk of text into their papers to make up the word count. I think this is not a good writing practice.

Paraphrasing is a better option in my opinion. That is, you should rewrite someone else's ideas in your own words to support your arguments or points. If you absolutely need to quote another person's thoughts directly in your paper, please limit it to only a few short sentences. Moreover, remember to show the year of publication and page number that the quote was originally shown in the article. Here is an example of a "Regular Quote" that is embedded in a paragraph:

> As Smith (2010) notes, "Canada is a multi-cultural society that is made up of people from all walks of life" (p. 78).

If your quote has more than 40 words in it, you need to use the "Block Quote" format. Here, you have to show the quote in a separate line, indent the left and right margins, make the font 1 or 2 size smaller, and use single line spacing like this:

> Customers with optimal rate plans are found to stay significantly longer with the wireless carrier than those with non-optimal ones. The author argues that wireless carriers should consider matching their customers to optimal rate plans for retention purpose (Wong, 2009, p. 73).

The citing and referencing styles that you are asked to follow by your professor or editor determine the exact way you cite. I will go over them with you in the latter part of this book.

Chapter 4 –
What are References?

A reference list refers to the complete list of referencing materials that appears at the end of your paper. Unlike a bibliography in which you include all of the materials that you have read while preparing your paper, a reference list shows only those resources that you have cited in your paper. Simply put:

- **Reference list**: list of cited materials in the paper. No more, no less.
- **Bibliography**: list of all reference materials, including those that you have read but have not cited in the paper.

In general, you should start your References section on a new page. Here is an example:

References

Atanasiu, V. and Smith, J. (2009), "Retailer's returns policies and competition," *Canadian Journal of Marketing Science*, 7 (1), 11-15.

Smith, J., Susan, M, and Kim, P. (2010), "Managing customer dissatisfaction: How to decrease opportunism by full refunds," *International Journal of Service Marketing*, 1 (3) 240-45.

List these resources in alphabetical order (based on the primary author's last name) in your reference section. The first one means that the paper titled "Retailer's returns policies and competition" is written by 2 authors. The primary author is Victor Atanasiu and the article is published in volume 7, issue 1 of the Canadian Journal of Marketing Science in 2009. The article appears from page 11 to 15.

Before you start preparing your reference section, it is important to understand what referencing style your professor or editor prefers. Read the next few sections to learn more about these different kinds of writing styles.

HOW ABOUT FOOTNOTES AND ENDNOTES?

"Don't use them, unless absolutely required." - Ken

Footnotes and Endnotes are alternative ways to identify the source of material used within your paper. You can also use them in explaining certain situations or difficult concepts. All you need to do is to place an Arabic numeral typed in superscript right after the text where you quote or make reference to another's work. Start with 1 and proceed to 2, 3…etc as far as needed. You can also use the "Insert footnote" function in most word processors if you don't want to manually insert the Roman numerals as superscript. Footnotes are placed at the bottom of each page while Endnotes are placed at the end of the paper. You should use either Footnotes or Endnotes but not both at the same time. Here is an example:

> These results comply with the data in Figure 5 for all the countries except Canada.[1]

At the bottom on the page, the footnote should show:

> [1] In Canada, the official languages are English and French while Chinese, Punjabi, Spanish, Italian and Dutch languages are also widely spoken.

If the footnotes/endnotes are used to identify the sources of referencing materials, full details should be shown in the initial citation.

[1] J. Smith (2010), Advanced Physics, UofT Press, Toronto, p.38.
[2] M. Susan (2010), Introduction to Biology, UofT Press, Toronto, p.12.

If the same material is being referred to immediately in the next footnote or endnote, you should use the word "ibid" which is the Latin word 'ibidem' meaning 'in the same place'. You do not need to show the author's name in this case:

[1] J. Smith (2010), Advanced Physics, UofT Press, Toronto, p.38.
[2] ibid., p.132.
[3] M. Susan (2010), Introduction to Biology, UofT Press, Toronto, p.12.

If the same material is being referred to in a later section of the paper (not immediately after the first citation), you should use the word "op.cit" which is the Latin word 'opere citato' meaning 'in the work cited.':

[1] J. Smith (2010), Advanced Physics, UofT Press, Toronto, p.38.
[2] M. Susan (2010), Introduction to Biology, UofT Press, Toronto, p.12.
[3] J. Smith, op.cit., p.132.

The use of footnotes and endnotes depends on the citing and referencing styles that you are subscribing to. Please refer to the following table to see the recommendations of each writing style on this matter:

Citing and Referencing Styles	Is the use of footnotes recommended?	Is the use of endnotes recommended?
APA	No	No
Chicago	Yes	Yes
Harvard	No	No

If you are submitting a manuscript to an academic journal, it is best to go over some of its previous volumes to see how other authors are treating their footnotes and/or endnotes, even if the journal is requiring the use of a particular citing and referencing styles. Remember that every journal has its own submission guidelines so you should read them carefully. If none of the articles make use of footnotes or endnotes in the journal, this writing practice is probably discouraged.

Chapter 5 –
Online Citation Generator and Software

"Dr. Wong, I don't have time to read through your book, is there a free tool that I can use NOW to help me put together the correct citing and referencing for my paper?"

The answer is "Yes" and there are some good tools that you can use. However, before you get too excited, bear in mind that you are relying on a 3rd party to do the work for you. While these online tools are great, I highly suggest that you learn the proper formats yourself because:

1. **It is simply faster.** Yes, it may take you a week or two to learn the proper citing and referencing style. But once you have acquired the skills, you can quickly and naturally write out the citations and references. Reliance on these online tools will require you to manually enter the information one-by-one, page-by-page, and going back-and-forth between your web browser and word processor.

2. **No need to worry about accuracy.** Although these online tools are quite good in general, how do you know if their back-end system will not break down tomorrow and give you some inaccurate results?

3. **Less distraction.** Perhaps it is just me. When I do my assignments, I don't like to be distracted by those online web banners and advertisements. Since these free online sites are all advertisement-sponsored, you will come across some banner ads when using their services.

FREE ONLINE CITATION GENERATORS

BibMe

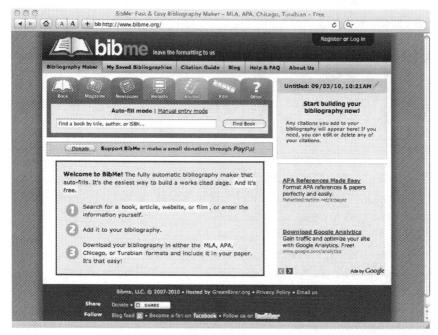

BibMe

http://www.bibme.org/

Launched in 2007, BibMe is an advertisement-sponsored online citation tool originated from a student project in the Carnegie Mellon University. This tool covers APA, Chicago and other formats. However, BibMe does not include the Harvard referencing style and it gives only referencing but not the in-text citation.

Step 1: Select type of article by clicking on the colorful tab (e.g. Journal)

Step 2: Click the "Manual entry mode" link

Step 3: Fill in the article details and click the "Add to my Bibliography" button.

Results from BibMe

Step 4: Select the format type in the pull down menu (e.g. APA) and then the corresponding citation will be shown.

Son of Citation Machine

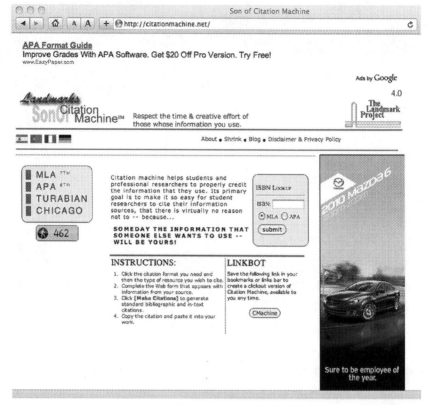

Son of Citation Machine

http://citationmachine.net/

Landmarks' Son of Citation Machine is another great advertisement-sponsored online tool. Similar to BibMe, it also covers both APA and Chicago formats. I like this one more because it includes both in-text citation and reference.

Step 1: Click the citing style on the left (e.g. APA 6th)
Step 2: Select type of article (e.g. Print --> Journal Article)
Step 3: Fill in the article details

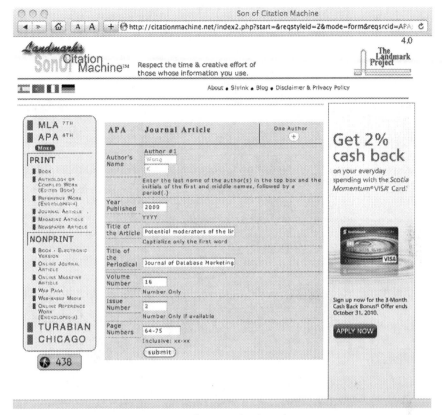

Enter the article details

Within a second, the correct parenthetical in-text citations and reference are shown.

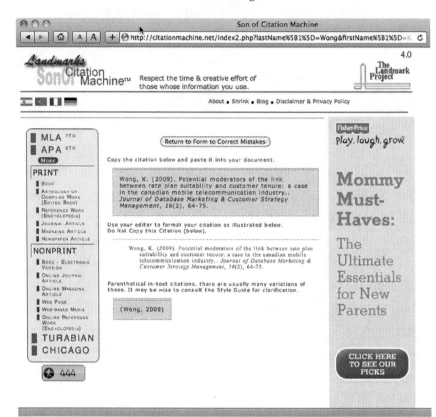

Results are shown

COMMERCIAL ONLINE CITATION GENERATORS

EasyBib

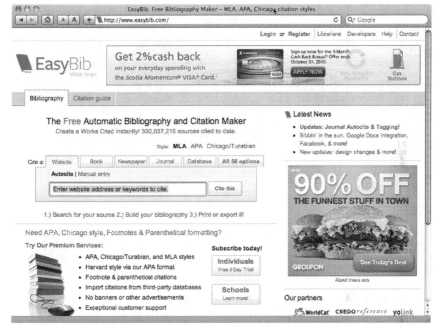

EasyBib

http://www.easybib.com/

EasyBib is a web-based online tool that helps students create citations in APA, Chicago and MLA styles. This online service targets colleges and universities, but individual users can also subscribe to the service on a monthly or annual basis. EasyBib covers both in-text citation and reference. MLA Citation services are provided free of charge while others are paid services.

RefWorks

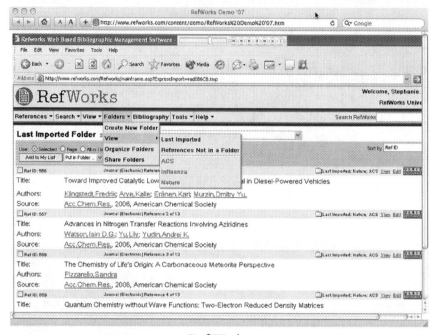

RefWorks

http://www.refworks.com

RefWorks is a web-based online citation tool that targets colleges and universities. Students should check with their school library to see if the library has already subscribed to the RefWorks service. In addition to helping students format their bibliography, the service also allows students to build a personal database to store their manuscripts and links. Detailed tutorials and user guides can be assessed through the provider's web site at http://www.refworks.com/content/quick_start_guide.asp.

COMMERCIAL CITATION SOFTWARE

EndNote

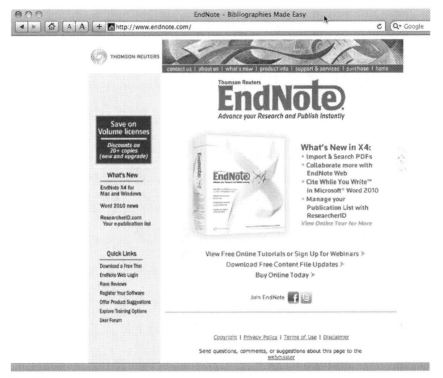

EndNote

http://www.endnote.com

EndNote is a commercial citation software that is published by Thomson Reuters. It works in conjunction with major word processing software such as Microsoft Word (Mac/PC) and Apple Pages (Mac). Similar to RefWorks, it does more than just citation creation for the writers. EndNote also has a web-based version known as EndNote Web that targets colleges and universities. Students are suggested to check with their school library to see if a campus-wide license is already available.

Chapter 6 – APA Style

APA stands for American Psychological Association (www.apa.org). If your professor asks you to use "APA Style" to write your paper, it means you should refer to the citing and referencing styles as detailed in the *Publication Manual of the American Psychological Association*. The 6th edition was published in 2009. By the time you read this book, APA may have the 7th or even the 8th edition available. Although each of these editions varies slightly, the basic rules are virtually the same. This section presents the key guidelines that you need for your writing. It is not meant to be a complete list and you should acquire the APA Publication Manual to learn more especially if you are responsible for page layout and formatting of a publication.

APA: Citations - One Author

First citation in text	Smith (2010)
Subsequent citations in text	Smith (2010)
Parenthetical format, first citation in text	(Smith, 2010)
Parenthetical format, subsequent citations in text	(Smith, 2010)

Note: Smith is the last name (i.e. surname) of the author.

APA: Citations - Two Authors for the Same Source

First citation in text	Smith and Susan (2010)
Subsequent citations in text	Smith and Susan (2010)
Parenthetical format, first citation in text	(Smith & Susan, 2010)
Parenthetical format, subsequent citations in text	(Smith & Susan, 2010)

Note: the "and" should be changed to "&" when using in a parenthetical format.

APA: Citations - Three to Five Authors for the Same Source

First citation in text	Smith, Susan and Kim (2010)
Subsequent citations in text	Smith et al. (2010)
Parenthetical format, first citation in text	(Smith, Susan, & Kim, 2010)
Parenthetical format, subsequent citations in text	(Smith et al., 2010)

Note: in some journals, editors like to have the "et al.," to be shown in italic type. For example, Smith et al. (2010) will be written as Smith *et al.* (2010).

APA: Citations - Six or More Authors for the Same Source

First citation in text	Smith et al. (2010)
Subsequent citations in text	Smith et al. (2010)
Parenthetical format, first citation in text	(Smith et al., 2010)
Parenthetical format, subsequent citations in text	(Smith et al., 2010)

APA: Citations - Organizational/Group Author

First citation in text	American Psychological Association (APA, 2010)
Subsequent citations in text	APA (2010)
Parenthetical format, first citation in text	(American Psychological Association [APA], 2010)
Parenthetical format, subsequent citations in text	(APA, 2010)

APA: Citations - No Author

Instead of using the author's last name, print the name of the article in quotation marks followed by the year of publication.

Example:

("History of Canada," 2010)

APA: Citations - Paraphrased Information

Examples:

Smith (2010) reported that 20% of Canadians have a language other than English or French as their mother tongue.

It has been found that Canadians drink 7 cups of coffee a week on average (Susan, 2010).

APA: Citations - Direct Quotes

Examples:

The CEO stated clearly that co-op students "needed manager's permission to access the company's data warehouse" (Smith, 2010, p. 15).

Susan (2011) stated that the "Proper background check needed to be implemented for new hires" (p. 18).

APA: Citations - Multiple Citations by the Same Author in Same Paragraph

Example:

A study by Smith and Susan (2010) found that the quality of the three sets of evaluation schemes were comparable. The subjective rubric developed by Smith and Susan helped to establish this. The study went on to show a difference between these MBA programs (Smith & Susan, 2009).

APA: Citations - Authors With the Same Last Name

If there are two or more authors with the same last name, always include the first author's initials in all text citations, even if the year of publication differs:

Reference List:

Kim, I. (2009). *Immigration: Networks, markets, and regulations in Ontario*. Toronto: UofT Press.

Kim, M. & Kim, K. (2011). The geographic expansion of Spanish immigration in Canada and its implications for local law enforcement. *Canadian Law Enforcement Journal*, 2, 77-80.

The citation in the text will then look like:

Among studies, we review M. Kim and Kim (2011) and I. Kim (2009).

APA: Citations - Multiple Authors for Different Source

If you are citing several representative sources for a key point, list the authors in alphabetical order within the same parentheses, and separate their names with semicolons. If the author's work is in still press (i.e. accepted by journal but not yet identified with the volume and issue of publication), write "in press" to replace the year of publication:

(Baurn & Benson, in press; Brydges & Smith, 2010; Wong, 1997; Zunderland & Li, 2007)

APA: Citations - Same Author for Different Source, Different Years

If you are citing several representative sources for a key point that are written by the same author in different years, you only need to show the author's last name once, and then list the year of publication for his/ her additional works. Show the earliest work first. Separate them with comma and not semicolons:

(Wong, 2001, 2009, in press)

APA: Citations - Same Author for Different Source, Same Year

If you are citing several representative sources for a key point that are written by the same author in the same year, you only need to show the author's last name once, and then add suffixes "a", "b", and "c"...etc after the year of publication to distinguish these references. Separate them with comma and not semicolons:

(Wong, 2009a, 2009b)

APA: Citations - Secondary Source

During your literature review, you may come across an article that includes a citation of another article that you cannot locate. It may be out-of-print, written in another language, or simply not available through the regular library access. Without reading the original article yourself, there is a risk to cite that source because you did not know about the context of the original paper. Having said that, if you strongly believe that you want to make reference to these materials, here's how you should do it:

Let's say Smith published an article in 1969 and it is subsequently cited in Wong's article in 2010. Assuming you did not read Smith's original work, you should:

1. In the text, write…according to Smith (as cited in Wong, 2010)
2. In the references section, list Wong's paper.

In other words, you cite the primary source in the text, and then list the secondary source in the references section.

APA: References - Book - One Author

Author's last name, first initial. (Year of publication). *Title of book in italic type*. Place of publication: Publisher.

If the author's first name is hyphenated (e.g. Kwong-Kay Wong), keep the hyphen and include a period after each initial.

Example:

Wong, K.-K. (2010). *The Academic Writing Guide*. New York, NY: Another University Press.

APA: References - Book - Same Author, Different Years

If the same author has written articles in different years, list them by year of publication with the earliest first.

Example:

Smith, D. (2002). *Hypotheses and facts*. New York, NY: Another University Press.

Smith, D. (2010). *Theory on children behavior*. New York, NY: Another University Press.

APA: References - Book - Same Author, Same Year, Different Months

Similar to citation, use suffixes "a", "b", "c", "d"…etc to distinguish one book from another.

Example:

Smith, D. (2010a). *Hypotheses and facts*. New York, NY: Another University Press.

Smith, D. (2010b). *Theory on children behavior*. New York, NY: Another University Press.

APA: References - Book - Two or More Authors

Author's last name, first initial. (Year). *Title of book*. Place of publication: Publisher.

Example:

Smith, G., & Kim, M. (2010). *Of course you're happy: a guide to deal with emotional challenges* (Rev. ed.). Toronto, ON: Another University Press.

Please note that one-author entries precede multiple-author entries, even if the multiple-author entries were published earlier:

Example:

Smith, D. (2010). *Hypotheses and facts*. New York, NY: Another University Press.

Smith, D. & Thomson, J. (1997). *Guide to Marketing*. New York, NY: Another University Press.

APA: References - Book - Organizational/Group Author

Organizational author. (Year). *Title of book*. Place of publication: Publisher.

Example:

American Children Association. (2010). *Children violence in America*. New York, NY: Another University Press.

If a Digital Object Identifier (DOI) is available with the book, please print it at the end, right after the publisher.

Example:

American Children Association. (2009). *Children violence in America*. New York, NY: Another University Press. doi:10/1013/30422-000

APA: References - Book - No Author

Title of book. (Year). Place of publication: Publisher.

Example:

The marketing handbook. (2010). New York, NY: Academic Press.

Note: If you can identify an organizational author for the book, use it instead. See previous example.

APA: References - Book - No Authors, Only Editors

Editor's last name, first initial. (Ed.). (Year). *Title of book*. Place of publication: Publisher.

Example:

Smith, P. & Wong, K. (Eds.). (2010). *Perspectives on children development*. Toronto, ON: Canadian University Press.

APA: References - Book - Edition Other Than the First

Author's last name, first initial. (Year). *Title of book*. (Number of edition). Place of publication: Publisher.

Example:

Smith, J. (2010). *Field guide to marketing* (2nd ed.). Toronto, ON: Canadian University Press.

Note: if the book is in its first edition, there is no need to show it.

APA: References - Book - Chapter or Article in an Edited Book

Author's last name, first initial. (Year). Title of Article. In Editor's first name initial and then editor's last name (Ed.), *Title of book*. (Volume number and then page number, if applicable). Place of publication: Publisher.

Example:

Smith, J. (2010). The Issue of Plagiarism. In S. Kim (Ed.), *Guide To Good Academic Writing* (Vol. 1, p. 207). Toronto, ON: Canadian University Press.

APA: References - Conference Proceedings (Officially Published)

Author's last name, first initial. (Year, Month). Title of paper. In Editor's first initial, last name (Ed.) *Title of Conference Proceedings*. (page numbers). Place of Publication: Publisher.

Example:

Smith, J. (2010). Impact of the e-learning platform on distance learner. In S. Wong (Ed.) *International Council for Distance Education Conference 2010* (pp. 179-185). Toronto, ON: Canadian University Press.

APA: References - Conference Presentations (Not Officially Published)

Author's last name, first initial. (Year, Month). Title of paper. In Chairperson first initial, last name (Chair), *Title of Conference.* Conference conducted at the meeting of Organization Name, Location.

Example:

Smith, J. R. (2010, May). Working with visually-challenged students: An integrated theoretical model. In J. S. Thomson (Chair), *Education in the 21st century.* Symposium conducted at the meeting of the Canadian Education Association World Conference, Toronto, ON.

APA: References - Data Set

Name of Data Set Provider. (Year). *Name of Data Set* [Data file]. Retrieved from URL of the Data Set.

Example:

Statistics Canada. (2010). *CENSUS 2006 Employment Report* [Data file]. Retrieved from http://www.statscan.gc.ca/datasets/1234567.html

APA: References - Dissertations and Theses - from ERIC Database

ERIC stands for the Educational Resources Information Center in the USA. If the dissertation is retrieved from its database, the reference format will look like:

Author's last name, first initial. (Year). *Title of dissertation.* (Doctoral dissertation). Retrieved from ERIC database. (ED code)

Example:

Smith, C. A. (2007). *Studying from remote provinces in Canada: A cross-sectional study.* (Doctoral dissertation.). Retrieved from ERIC database. (ED4123967)

APA: References - Dissertations and Theses - from ProQuest

Author's last name, first initial. (Year). *Title of dissertation*. Available from Database Name. (Dissertation identification code)

Example:

Smith, S. (2010). *Mergers and Acquisitions: Evidence from Canadian Banks*. Available from ProQuest Dissertations and Theses database. (UMI No. 123456)

APA: References - Dissertations and Theses - from Institutional Database

Author's last name, first initial. (Year). *Title of dissertation*. (Doctoral dissertation). Retrieved from URL of database.

Example:

Smith, J. (2010). *Model for Strategic Marketing in the Banking Sector*. (Doctoral dissertation). Retrieved from http://www.utoronto.ca/etd/phd12345.html

APA: References - Encyclopedia or Dictionary (Online)

Author's last name, first initial. (n.d. which stands for no date). Entry heading. In *Title of encyclopedia* (volume number and then page number, if applicable. Otherwise, use edition information). Retrieved from URL

Example:

Smith, C. (n.d.). Shopaholic syndrome. In *Canadian Women Encyclopedia* (Fall 2010 ed.). Retrieved from http://www.utoronto.ca/entries12346

APA: References - Encyclopedia or Dictionary (Print)

Entry heading (Year). In *Title of encyclopedia* (volume number and then page number, if applicable). Place of publication: Publisher.

Example:

Social Networking. (2010). In *New Canadian dictionary* (3rd ed.). Toronto, ON: Another University Press.

APA: References - Google Books (Online)

Author's last name, first initial. (Year). Title of work. Place of publication: Publisher. Retrieved from URL (Original work published in YEAR)

Example:

Smith, J. (2010). International Marketing. New York, NY: Another University Press. Retrieved from http://books.google.com/books12345. html (Original work published in 1985)

Note: The 2010 refers to the year the ebook becomes available. The 1985 refers to the original publication year of the printed copy.

APA: References - Personal Communications

According to APA, any type of private, personal communications conducted by researcher should only be citied in the text of the paper. There is no need to show it in the list of references.

APA: References - Telephone Interview

Interviewee's last name, first initial. (Year of interview). A telephone interview with name of interviewee's first name and last name/ Interviewer: Interviewer's first name and last name. Title of the discussion topic. Name of the organization that the Interviewee is affiliated with, Place.

Example:

Let's say John Smith officially interviewed me over the phone, it will look like this as per APA style:

Wong, K. (2010). A telephone interview with Dr. Ken Wong/Interviewer: John Smith. Marketing strategies for Female Executives. University of Toronto, Ontario.

APA: References - Journal Article with DOI assigned.

Author last name, first initial. (Year). Title of article. *Title of journal.* Volume number(issue number), page numbers. DOI information.

Example:

Smith, J. (2010). Brand Extension Strategy for Japanese Brands. *Journal of International Marketing,* 32(2), 50-52. doi:20.1022/0202-1232.77.4.321

APA: References - Journal Article - Retrieved from an Online Subscription Database

Author's last name, first initial. (Year). Title of article. *Title of journal.* Volume number(issue number), page numbers. Retrieved from home page URL for the journal.

Example:

Smith, T.-J., Jr. (2010). Information literacy for home schoolers. *International Journal of Library Management,* 32(4), 50-52. Retrieved from http://www.library.org/article12345.html

If the journal has ceased to exist and/or there's no home page for the journal, use the name of database instead.

Example:

Smith, B. (1923). The experience of a junior high principal. *Journal of School Management*, 3, 7. Retrieved from JSTOR database.

APA: References - Journal Article - (Printed Version)

Author's last name, first initial & second author's last name, first initial. (Year). Title of article. *Title of journal*. Volume number(issue number), page numbers.

Example:

Smith, J. & Susan, M. (2010). Branding strategies for Canadian firms. *International Journal of Marketing*, 24(3), 14-20.

APA: References - Magazine - No Author

Title of article. (Publication date). *Title of magazine*. Volume (issue), page range.

Example:

All You Need to Know About RRSP and RESP. (2010, September). *Canadian Financial Magazine*, 30(2), 5-7.

APA: References - Magazine - One Author

Author's last name, first initials. (Publication date). Title of article. *Title of magazine*, Volume (issue), page range.

Example:

Smith, J.R. (2010, July 10). Marketing in the 21st Century. *Canadian Business Magazine*, 190 (2), 63-67.

APA: References - Newspaper (Online)

Author's last name, first initial. (Publication year, month and day). Title of article. *Name of newspaper.* Retrieved from URL.

Example:

Smith, T. S. (2010, February 15). The 911 Incident Re-Visited. *New York Times.* Retrieved from http://www.nytimes.com/2010/23e1341f5.html

APA: References - Newspaper (Print)

Author's last name, first name. (Publication year, month and day). Title of article. *Name of newspaper.* pp. section or name.

Example:

Smith, John (2010, March 30). Do we need the long Census form?. *The Globe and Mail.* pp. B2.

APA: References - Online Communities (Blogs, Forums, Newsgroups, Social Networking Sites)

Author's last name, first initial. (year, date). Thread Title [Message type]. Retrieved from URL of the message.

Example:

Smith, J. F. (2010, May 2). Problems of Facebook [Online forum comment]. Retrieved from http://groups.google.com/group/facebook/12345.html

APA: References - Recordings (DVDs, CDs, Tape)

Producer's last name, first initial. (Producer), Director last name, first initial (Director). (Year of release). *Title.* [Medium of recording]. Country of origin: Studio.

Example:

Smith, J. (Producer), & Thompson, S. (Director). (2010). *The Twin Tower Story* [DVD]. Toronto, ON: Universal ABC Video.

APA: References - Specialized Software with Limited Distribution

Author's last name, first initial. (Date). Title of software or computer program (Version number) [Any identifier]. City, state: Name of producer. Retrieved from URL

Example:

Smith, C., Will, S., and Wayne, T. (2010). SmartPLS 1.0 (beta) Hamburg, Germany: University of Hamburg. Retrieved from http://www.smartpls.de.

APA: References - Technical and Research Reports (Online)

Author's last name, first initial. (Year). *Title of publication.* (Report number). Retrieved from name of institution: URL of the report.

Example:

Smith, F. D., Kim, R., & Wong, A. (2010). *Populations of the Caribbean, 2009.* (Report No. 1234567). Retrieved from Statistic Bureau of the Caribbean web site: http://www.statisticcaribbean.org/pubs2009/2009RL1234567.pdf

If the author is unknown, treat the government department or agency as the group author.

Example:

National Center for Census, Statistics Canada (2010). *Statistical analysis report: Ethical income level* (SC 10-2345). Retrieved from http://www.statscan.gc.ca/pubs/102345.html

APA: References - Unpublished Academic Paper Retrieved Online

Author's last name, first initial. (Year of publication, or "n.d." for no date). *Title of article.* Unpublished manuscript. Name of Institution, Program and/or Department. Retrieved from URL of the online article

Example:

Smith, J. C. (n.d.). *Comparisons of school performance between boys and girls in the 12-20 age group.* Unpublished manuscript. Programs for Children Education, Faculty of Arts and Science, University of Toronto. Retrieved from http://www.utoronto.ca/phd /phd/online_documents. htm

APA: References - Web Article without Author

Title of article. (Year of publication, edition name or publication date). *Title of the web site.* Retrieved from URL of the online article.

Example:

Citizen Mobility in The Middle East. (2010, spring). *The Mirror: Newsletter of the Another University.* Retrieved from http://www. anotheruniversity.edu/themirror/newsletter/Spring2010.pdf

APA: References - Web Article with Author

Author's last name, first initial. (Year of publication, edition name or publication date). Title of article. *Title of the web site.* Retrieved from URL of the online article.

Example:

Smith, T. (2010, May 2). What has to be changed at Facebook? *PC World.* Retrieved from http://www.salon.com/2010/05/02/facebook/ index.html

APA: References - YouTube Video

Author's last name, first initial. (year, date). File Name [Video file]. Retrieved from URL of the video clip.

Example:

Smith, J. A. (2010, August 6). The Unboxing of my Apple iPad [Video file]. Retrieved from http://www.YouTube.com/group/watch?v=TGJ7h43nsu_Id

Note: The title of the video is not italicized.

Chapter 7 –
Chicago Style

The Chicago citing and referencing styles are commonly used in publications written in American English. If your professor asks you to use "Chicago Style" to write your paper, it means you should refer to the citing and referencing styles as detailed in *The Chicago Manual of Style* that is published by the University of Chicago Press. The information presented here is based on the 16th edition that was published in 2010. By the time you read this book, Chicago may have the 17th or even the 18th edition available. Although each of these editions varies slightly, the basic rules are virtually the same. Technically speaking, there are two basic documentation systems within the Chicago Style:

1. **Humanities Style** (a.k.a. Documentary Notes Style, Notes and Bibliography Style, or NB Style). It is common in Arts, Literature and History disciplines

2. **Author-Date System**. It is common in science and business disciplines.

Since this book is written for my business students, I am going to show you the Author-Date System of the Chicago Style that you will use for your marketing papers. This chapter presents the key guidelines that you need for your writing. It is not meant to be a complete list, and you should acquire *The Chicago Manual of Style* to learn more—especially if you are responsible for page layout and formatting of a publication.

Chicago: Citations - One Author

First citation in text	Smith (2007)
Subsequent citations in text	Smith (2007)
Parenthetical format, first citation in text	(Smith 2007)
Parenthetical format, subsequent citations in text	(Smith 2007)

Note: Smith is the last name of the author

Notes:
Unlike APA, Chicago style does not use a comma to separate the author last name and the year of publication. A space between them is sufficient.

Also, page numbers or other specific references may be omitted in citations to journal articles unless you are showing direct quotations. If these specific references have to be shown, they should look like this:

Smith (2007, 12)
(Smith 2007, 12)
(Smith and Johnson, sec. 30)
(Smith 2007, 2:456-58, 3:20)
(Smith 2007, under "The Country") [an unpaginated electronic work]

Chicago: Citations - Two Authors for the Same Source

First citation in text	Smith and Thomas (2007)
Subsequent citations in text	Smith and Thomas (2007)
Parenthetical format, first citation in text	(Smith and Thomas 2007)
Parenthetical format, subsequent citations in text	(Smith and Thomas 2007)

Note: Please use "and" instead of "&". You will also realize that unlike APA style, there's no comma between the last name and the year of publication.

Chicago: Citations - Three Authors for the Same Source

First citation in text	Smith, Wong and Thomas (2007)
Subsequent citations in text	Smith, Wong and Thomas (2007)
Parenthetical format, first citation in text	(Smith, Wong and Thomas 2007)
Parenthetical format, subsequent citations in text	(Smith, Wong and Thomas 2007)

Chicago: Citations - Four or More Authors for the Same Source

First citation in text	Smith et al. (2007)
Subsequent citations in text	Smith et al. (2007)
Parenthetical format, first citation in text	(Smith et al. 2007)
Parenthetical format, subsequent citations in text	(Smith et al. 2007)

Note:

"et al." is NOT italicized in Chicago style. You can also use "and others" instead of "et al." this way:

In a study by Wong and others (2009), ...

Chicago: Citations - Organizational/Group Author

First citation in text	American Psychological Association (2010)
Subsequent citations in text	American Psychological Association (2010)
Parenthetical format, first citation in text	(American Psychological Association 2010)
Parenthetical format, subsequent citations in text	(American Psychological Association 2010)

Chicago: Citations - No Author

If no author is listed, use "Anon." in the text citation followed by the year of publication.

Example:

(Anon. 2009)

Chicago: Citations - Paraphrased Information

Examples:

Wong (2010, 49) reported that the number of immigrants in Ontario has increased significantly since 2008…

Kim's study (2009) indicates that…

The decision to eliminate the Long Form in Census has been heavy criticized by the Canadian economists (Wong 2010).

Chicago: Citations - Direct Quotes

Examples:

The headmaster stated clearly that pupils "needed teacher's permission to use the lab computer for facebooking" (Smith 2010, 78).

Smith (2010, 74) stated that the "Vancouver is ranked by the UN as the best city to live in North America".

Chicago: Citations - Multiple Citations by the Same Author in Same Paragraph

Only one parenthetical citation is needed, and it can be placed after the last reference, or at the end of the paragraph. However, if the page number of the source being cited is different, text citation should be included after each reference.

Example:

A study by Smith and Kim (2010, 39) found that tech-savvy students tend to commit plagiarism. The anti-plagiarism software developed by Smith and Kim helped to verify this claim. The study went on to show a difference between MBA programs (Smith and Kim 2010, 42).

Chicago: Citations - Authors With the Same Last Name

If there are two or more authors with the same last name, always include the first author's initials in all text citations, even if the year of publication differs:

Reference List:

Smith, Ivan. 2010. Networks, markets, and regulations in Canada. Toronto, ON: Another University Press.

Smith, Mike. and John Kim. 2008. The geographic expansion of Chinese immigration in Canada. RCMP Forum Journal, 2, 64-77.

The citation in the text will then look like:

Among studies, we review M. Smith and J. Kim (2008) and I. Smith (2010).

Chicago: Citations - Multiple Authors for Different Source

If you are citing several representative sources for a key point, list the authors in alphabetical order within the same parentheses, and separate their names with semicolons. If the author's work is in still press (i.e. accepted by journal but not yet identified with the volume and issue of publication), write "in press" to replace the year of publication:

(Smith and Kim in press; Smith and Lee 2007; Wong 2010)

Chicago: Citations - Same Author for Different Source, Different Years

If you are citing several representative sources for a key point that are written by the same author in different years, you only need to show the author's last name once, and then list the year of publication for his/ her additional works. Show the earliest work first. Separate them with comma and not semicolons:

(Wong 2008, 2010)

Chicago: Citations - Same Author for Different Source, Same Year

If you are citing several representative sources for a key point that are written by the same author in the same year, you only need to show the author's last name once, and then add "a", "b", and "c" after the year of publication to distinguish them from each other. Separate them with comma and not semicolons:

(Wong 2009a, 2009b)

Chicago: Citations - Secondary Source

During your literature review, you may come across an article that includes a citation of another article that you cannot locate. It may be out-of-print, written in another language, or simply not available through the regular library access. Without reading the original article yourself, there is a risk to cite that source because you did not know about the context of the original paper. Having said that, if you strongly believe that you want to make reference to these materials, you should cite the original article in the text, and then list both original and secondary sources in the reference list.

Let's say Smith published an article in 1978 and it is subsequently cited in Johnston's article in 2010. Assuming you did not read Smith's original work, you should:

1. In the text, write…according to Smith (1978)

2. In the references section, list both papers and cross-reference them:

References

Smith, John. 1978. Title of Original Paper. *Title of Original Journal.* 134-160. Cambridge, MA: Harvard Univ. Press. Quoted in Johnston 2010, 230-233.

Johnston, Tom. 2010. Title of Secondary Paper. Title of Secondary Journal. 230-233. Toronto, ON: Another University Press.

Chicago: References - Book - One Author

Author's last name, first name. Year of publication. *Title of book including subtitle in italic type.* Place of publication: Publisher.

Example:

Smith, David. 2009. *Hypotheses and facts.* Toronto, ON: Another University Press.

If the same author has written articles in different years, list them by year of publication with the earliest first.

Example:

Smith, David. 2009. *Hypotheses and facts.* Toronto, ON: Another University Press.

Smith, David. 2010. *Theory on children behavior.* Toronto, ON: Another University Press.

Note: In general, we should show the author's first name and not the first initial in a reference list. However, there are some books or journals that prefer to use first initials so please check with the editor. The latter will look like this:

Smith, D. 2010. *Theory on children behavior.* Toronto, ON: Another University Press.

Chicago: References - Book - Same Author, Different Years

List the earliest work first. Subsequent work should use the "3-EM" dash (i.e. six hyphens as a solid line) for repeated names. This applies to journal entries as well. [Tips: Press Ctrl+Alt+Hypen in PC's Microsoft Word, or Shift+Option+Hypen in Mac's Microsoft Word to get the EM dash. You may also need to change the font to something like Arial to see a smooth 3-EM dash without breakage]

Example:

Smith, D. 2009. *Hypotheses and facts.* Toronto, ON: Another University Press.

————. 2010. *Title of a book.* Los Angeles, CA: Jimmy Press.

————. 2011. *Title of another book.* Toronto, ON: University of Toronto Press.

Chicago: References - Book - Same Author, Same Year

Similar to citation, use suffixes "a", "b", "c", "d"…etc to distinguish one book from another.

Example:

Smith, David. 2009a. *Hypotheses and facts.* Toronto, ON: Another University Press

————. 2009b. *Title of a book.* San Francisco, CA: Academic Press.

Chicago: References - Book - Two to Ten Authors

Primary author's last name, first name, middle initial (if applicable). Second author's first name, last name, middle initial (if applicable).

Third author's first name, last name, middle initial (if applicable). Year. *Title of book*. Place of publication: Publisher.

Note: This means that if 10 authors write the book, you have to list all of their names in the reference list.

Example:

Wong, Ken, John Smith, and Mary Susan. 2010. *A guide to dealing with personal relationships* (Rev. ed.). Toronto, ON: Another University Press.

Please note that one-author entries precede multiple-author entries, even if the multiple-author entries were published earlier:

Example:

Smith, David. 2009. *Hypotheses and facts*. Toronto, ON: Another University Press.

Smith, David, and John Smith. 2001. *Example of Another Book Title*. New York, NY: Academic Press.

Chicago: References - Book - Eleven or More Authors

If more than 10 authors write the book, list the names of the first seven authors and then followed by "et al."

Example:

Wong, Ken, John Smith, Mary Susan, Peter Wong, Kim Chan, Tony Jar, Steve Jobs et al. 2010. *Example of Book Title*. New York, NY: Another University Press.

Chicago: References - Book - Organizational/Group Author

Group author. Year. *Title of book*. Place of publication: Publisher.

Example:

American Children Association. 2010. *School bullying in North America*. New York, NY: Another University Press.

Chicago: References - Book - No Author

Anon. Year. *Book Title*. Place of publication: Publisher.

Example:

Anon. 2010. *The marketing strategy handbook*. Vancouver, BC: Academic Press.

Chicago: References - Book - No Authors, Only Editors

Primary editor's last name, first name, Second editor's first name, last name, eds. Year. *Title of book*. Place of publication: Publisher.

Example:

Smith, Peter, ed. 2009. *Marketing Strategies for Non-Profits*. Chicago, IL: American Marketing Association.

Smith, Peter, Ken Wong, and John Smith, eds. 2010. *Direct Marketing and Social Networking*. Toronto, ON: Canadian Marketing Association.

Note: The same format applies to Translator (tran), Translators (trans), Compiler (comp) and Compilers (comps).

Chicago: References - Book - Edition Other Than the First

Author's last name, first name. Year. *Title of book*. Number of edition. Place of publication: Publisher.

Example:

Smith, John. 2010. *Field guide for mobile marketing professionals.* 3rd ed. Toronto, ON: Another University Press.

Note: if the book is in its first edition, there is no need to show it.

Chicago: References - Book - Chapter or Article in an Edited Book

Author's last name, first name. Year. Title of article. In *Title of book,* Edition, ed. Editor first name and last name, page numbers. Place of publication: Publisher.

Example:

Wong, Ken. 2010. The demise of Second Life. In *Strategic Marketing Tactics,* 3rd edition, ed. Mary Susan, 107-111. Toronto, ON: Canadian University Press.

Chicago: References - Conference Proceedings (Officially Published)

First author's last name, first name, second author's first name, last name. Year. Title of paper. In Editor's first initial, last name, ed. *Title of Conference Proceedings.* page numbers. Place of Publication: Publisher

Example:

Lee, Thomas, John Smith. 2010. Impact of Internet technology on distance learning. In *Canadian Council for Distance Education,* ed. M. Wong , 179-183. Toronto, ON: Another University Press.

Chicago: References - Conference Presentations (Not Officially Published)

First author's last name, first name, second author's first name, last name. Year. Title of paper. Paper presented at the Title of Conference. Conference, Location.

(Please note that for unpublished works, the title of the paper should NOT be printed in italic)

Example:

Smith, John, and Thomas Lee. 2010. The issue of plagiarism in Canadian colleges. Paper presented at the annual meeting of the Canadian Educator Association, Toronto.

Chicago: References - Data Set

If there's an author, show name of data set author. Year. Name of Data set. Name of data provider. Access date. URL.

Example:

Smith, J. 2010. *Income Level Survey in Ontario*. Statistics Canada. Data set accessed 2010-03-14 at http://www.statcan.gc.ca/data/123456. html.

If there's no author, show name of database, URL ([data set name or identifier]; access date).

Example:

Income Level Survey. http://www.statcan.gc.ca/Incomelevel/123.html (for IL11-321234 [accession number BC123456]; accessed August 29, 2010)

Chicago: References - Dissertations and Theses - from ERIC Database

ERIC stands for the Educational Resources Information Center in the USA. If the dissertation is retrieved from its database, the reference format will look like:

Author's last name, first initial. Year. Title of dissertation.. PhD diss.,

Name of University. Retrieved from ERIC database (ED code) (access date)

Example:

Smith, J. 2010. Corporate Governance in Canadian-based MNC. PhD diss. University of Toronto. Retrieved from ERIC database. (ED12345) (accessed Jan 6, 2010).

Chicago: References - Dissertations and Theses - from ProQuest

Author's last name, first initial. Year. Title of dissertation. PhD diss., Name of University. Available from Database Name. (Dissertation identification code) (access date).

Example:

Smith, J. 2010. Corporate Governance in Canadian-based MNC. PhD diss. University of Toronto. Available from ProQuest Dissertations and Theses database. (UMI No. 1234567) (accessed Jan 3, 2010).

Chicago: References - Dissertations and Theses - from Institutional Database

Author's last name, first initial. Year. Title of dissertation. PhD diss., Name of University. URL. (access date).

Example:

Smith, J. 2010. Corporate Governance in Canadian-based MNC. PhD diss. University of Toronto. http://www.vtu.edu/etd/ (accessed Jan 3, 2010).

Chicago: References - Encyclopedia or Dictionary (Online)

Title of encyclopedia, s.v. (*sub verbo*, "under the word") "Entry heading," (by Author's First Name, Last Name if applicable), URL (accessed date).

Example:

The New Canadian Dictionary of Computer, s.v. "Cloud Computing" (by John Smith), http://www.canadiancomputerdictionary.ca/ (accessed January 3, 2010).

Chicago: References - Encyclopedia or Dictionary (Print)

Title of Famous encyclopedia, edition number, s.v. "Entry heading."

(please note that it's common to cite reference works in notes rather than in bibliographies)

Example:

Encyclopedia Britannica, 16th., s.v. "Globalization."

If the reference work is not so popular, full details of the publication has to be provided.

Example:

Smith, John. 2007. *John's modern netique guide.* Toronto, ON: Another University Press.

Chicago: References - Google Books (Online)

Author's last name, first name. Year. Title of work. Place of publication: Publisher. URL (accessed date).

Example:

Smith, John. 1963. The invention of Telephone. Chicago, IL: Academic Press. http://books.google.com/books/12345.html (accessed December 2, 2009).

Chicago: References - Interview or Personal Communications

Last name of person interviewed, first name. Year of interview. Interview by name of interviewer. Brief identifying information. The place and date of interview.

Example:

Wong, Ken. 2010. Interview by John Smith. Tape recording. July 10. University of Toronto, ON.

Chicago: References - Journal Article with DOI assigned.

Author's last name, first initial. Second author's first initial last name. Year. Title of article. *Title of journal.* Volume number(month of publication): DOI information.

Example:

Smith, J., and M. Susan. 2010. Branding strategies for Canadian firms. *International Journal of Marketing*, 24(Mar). doi:20.1022/1234-9822.77.4.321

Chicago: References - Journal Article - Retrieved from an Online Subscription Database

Author's last name, first initial. Second author's first initial last name. Year. Title of article. *Title of journal.* Volume number(month of publication): page number. URL. (access date).

Example:

Smith, J., and M. Susan. 2010. Branding strategies for Canadian firms. *International Journal of Marketing*, 24(Mar): 14-20. http://www.journalofmarketing.com/12345.html. (accessed Jan 5, 2010).

Chicago: References - Journal Article - (printed version)

Author last name, first initial. Second author's first initial last name. Year. Title of article. *Title of journal.* Volume number(month of publication): page number.

Example:

Smith, J., and M. Susan. 2010. Branding strategies for Canadian firms. *International Journal of Marketing*, 24(Mar): 14-20.

Chicago: References - Magazine - No Author

If there's no author, use the name of the magazine.

Magazine name. Year of publication. Article title. Month of publication.

Example:

PC World. 2005. Titanium Notebook for Mobile Professional. June.

Chicago: References - Magazine - One Author

Author's last name, first name. Year of publication. Article title. Magazine title, Month of publication.

Example:

Smith, John. 2010. The quest for water in desert. Scientific American, May.

Chicago: References - Newspaper (Online)

Author's last name, first name. Year of publication. Title of article. *Name of newspaper.* Publication date. Section name. URL (access date).

Example:

Smith, John. 2010. Good reasons to have the long census form. *Toronto Star*, July 26, Business section. http://www.thestar.com/2010/33e1341. html (accessed Aug 1, 2010)

Chicago: References - Newspaper (Print)

Author's last name, first name. Year of publication. Title of article. *Name of newspaper*. Publication date, section name, edition name.

Example:

Smith, John. 2010. Good reasons to have the long census form. *Toronto Star*, July 26, Business section. GTA edition.

Chicago: References - Online Communities (Blogs, Forums, Newsgroups, Social Networking Sites)

Name of the Blog. URL. (access date).

Example:

John-Smith blog, The. http://johnsmith123.blogspot.com/ (accessed May 3, 2010).

Chicago: References - Recordings (DVDs, CDs, Tape)

Producer's last name, first name, Director first name last name. *Title*. Medium of recording. Country of origin: Studio, Year of release.

Example:

Lee, Tom and John Smith. *The Opening Ceremony of the Beijing Olympics* [DVD]. Toronto, ON: Universal Video, 2008.

Chicago: References - Specialized Software with Limited Distribution

Author's last name, first initial. *Title of software or computer program* (Version number) [Any identifier]. Media Type. Name of producer. Year of publication. If the media is downloadable, show URL.

Example:

Ringle, C., Wende, S., and Will A. *SmartPLS 2.0 (beta)*. Downloadable Software. University of Hamburg, 2002. Retrieved from http://www.smartpls.de.

Chicago: References - Technical and Research Reports (Online)

Author's last name, first initial. Second author's first initial, last name. Year. *Title of publication*. (Report number). Retrieved from name of institution: URL of the report. (access date)

Example:

Smith, J., K., Wong, and T. Lee. 2010. *Population Change in Canada, 2010*. (Report No. ABC12345). Retrieved from Statistics Canada website: http://www.statcan.gc.ca/pubs2016/2010AABC12345.pdf (accessed Aug 4, 2010).

If the author is unknown, treat the government department or agency as the group author.

Example:

Survey Group, Statistics Canada. 2010. *Population Change in Canada, 2010*. (Report No. ABC12345). Retrieved from http://www.statcan.gc.ca/pubs2016/2010AABC12345.pdf (accessed Aug 4, 2010).

Chicago: References - Unpublished Academic Paper Retrieved Online

Author's last name, first initial. Year or publication. Title of article. Unpublished manuscript (or Working paper), Name of Institution, Program and/or Department. URL (access date)

Example:

Smith, J. T. 2000. Comparisons of students performance in the 18-25 age group. Working paper, Programs for Higher Education, Faculty of Education, University of Toronto. Retrieved from http://www.utoronto. ca/phd/online_documents123.htm (accessed Jan 15, 2010).

Chicago: References - Web Article without Author

Organization or Group Author. Year of publication. Title of the Article. *Title of Website*. If applicable, name of any Sponsoring Institution/ Organization associated with the Website. URL (access date)

Example:

The Internet Survey Group. 2010. Use of social networking for marketing among SMBs. The Canadian Marketer's Corner. Canadian Marketing Association http://www.canadianmarketers.ca/library/doc-123.html (accessed May 9, 2010)

Chicago: References - Web Article with Author

Author's Last Name, First Name. Year of publication. Title of the Article. *Title of Website*. If applicable, name of any Sponsoring Institution/ Organization associated with the Website. URL (access date)

Example:

Smith, John. 2010. Mobility in developing world. *Mirror of the world: Newsletter of Another University.* http://www.another.edu/portalsoftheworld/newsletter2010/2010Winter.pdf (accessed July 21, 2010).

Chicago: References - YouTube Video

Author's last name, first initial. Year of publication. *File Name, Video file. URL. (access date).*

Example:

Smith, J. 2010. The iPhone 4 antenna problem [Video file]. http://www.YouTube.com/group/watch?v=Xsfww3su_IRB (accessed Aug 5, 2010)

Chapter 8 –
Harvard Style

The Harvard Referencing Style (a.k.a. author-date style or Parenthetical referencing) is a citing and referencing method that is very popular among academics in Australia, UK and South Africa. Contrary to popular belief, this referencing style is not developed or endorsed by Harvard University, although it originated from the referencing techniques used by Edward Laurens Mark (1847-1946), who was the Hersey professor of anatomy and director of Harvard's zoological laboratory. In fact, MBA students from Harvard Business School are asked to follow the HBS Citation Guide that is based on the Chicago style.

To learn more about the history of the "Harvard" style, see the article titled "The "Harvard System": A mystery dispelled" that is written by Eli Chernin in Vol. 297 (22 Oct 1988), page 1062-1063 of British Medical Journal. http://www.bmj.com/cgi/pdf_extract/297/6655/1062

Unlike the APA and Chicago styles that are being centrally managed and updated by their corresponding publisher, the Harvard style has no publisher. It has been gradually evolved since 1881 (when Professor Mark first used it in his journal article) as this style started to gain acceptance among the academic communities around the world. As a result, each university may have its own interpretation of the Harvard style and my opinion is that you should simply follow the version that your university or journal is suggesting. In this section, I'm going to show you the Harvard style that is used by Imperial College London in UK, so don't be alarmed to find slight difference of what I'm writing as compared to those that you find on the Internet. See more at:

http://www3.imperial.ac.uk/library/subjectsandsupport/
referencemanagement/harvard

Harvard: Citations - One Author

First citation in text	Smith (2007)
Subsequent citations in text	Smith (2007)
Parenthetical format, first citation in text	(Smith, 2007)
Parenthetical format, subsequent citations in text	(Smith, 2007)

Note: Smith is the last name of the author

Harvard: Citations - Two Authors for the Same Source

First citation in text	Smith and Thomas (2007)
Subsequent citations in text	Smith and Thomas (2007)
Parenthetical format, first citation in text	(Smith & Thomas, 2007)
Parenthetical format, subsequent citations in text	(Smith & Thomas, 2007)

Note: the "and" should be changed to "&" when using in a parenthetical format.

Harvard: Citations - Three or More Authors for the Same Source

First citation in text	Smith, Thomas and Jones (2007)
Subsequent citations in text	Smith et al (2007)
Parenthetical format, first citation in text	(Smith, Thomas, & Jones, 2007)
Parenthetical format, subsequent citations in text	(Smith et al, 2007)

Note: in some journals, editors like to have the "et al," to be shown in italic type. For example, Smith et al. (2007) will be written as Smith *et al* (2007). Meanwhile, some journals like to add a dot after "et al" to make it "et al." or "*et al.*". These are minor differences and you should not be too concerned about them.

Harvard: Citations - Author from an Edited Book

First citation in text	Smith (2007)
Subsequent citations in text	Smith (2007)
Parenthetical format, first citation in text	(Smith, 2007)
Parenthetical format, subsequent citations in text	(Smith, 2007)

An edited book may include chapters written by different authors. When citing work from this kind of book, you should cite the chapter author(s) and not the book editor.

Harvard: Citations - Organizational/Group Author

First citation in text	Toronto Transit Commission (TTC, 2010)
Subsequent citations in text	Toronto Transit Commission (2010)
Parenthetical format, first citation in text	(Toronto Transit Commission [TTC], 2010)
Parenthetical format, subsequent citations in text	(TTC, 2010)

Note: Always show the full name of the organization in the first citation. If there's a commonly known short form such as TTC in this example, include it in [ ] as part of the first citation so that you can just print the short form in subsequent citations.

Harvard: Citations - No Author

Use "Anon" as the author name followed by the year of publication.

Example:

(Anon, 2009)

Note: You're strongly suggested not to reference material that has no author. Think about it, it's like quoting someone's thoughts that you heard on the street and you don't know who he/she is. Can you really trust this information?

Harvard: Citations - Paraphrased Information

Examples:

Smith (2010) reported that 20% of Canadians have a language other than English or French as their mother tongue.

It has been found that Canadians drink 7 cups of coffee a week on average (Susan, 2010).

Harvard: Citations - Direct Quotes

Examples:

The CEO stated clearly that co-op students "needed manager's permission to access the company's data warehouse" (Smith, 2010:p.15).

Susan stated that the "Proper background check needed to be implemented for new hires" (2010:p.18).

Note: page number must be shown. Double quotation marks are used for quoting direct speech.

Harvard: Citations - Multiple Citations by the Same Author in Same Paragraph

Example:

A study by Smith and Susan (2010) found that the quality of the three sets of evaluation schemes were comparable. The subjective rubric developed by Smith and Susan helped to establish this. The study went on to show a difference between these MBA programs (Smith & Susan, 2009).

Harvard: Citations - Authors With the Same Last Name

If there are two or more authors with the same last name, always include the author's initials in all text citations, even if the year of publication differs:

Reference List:

Kim, I. (2009) *Immigration: Networks, markets, and regulations in Ontario.* Toronto, ON, UofT Press.

Kim, M. & Kim, K. (2011) The geographic expansion of Spanish immigration in Canada and its implications for local law enforcement. *Canadian Law Enforcement Journal,* 2, 77-80.

The citation in the text will then look like:

Among studies, we review M. Kim and Kim (2011) and I. Kim (2009).

Harvard: Citations - Multiple Authors for Different Source

If you are citing several representative sources for a key point, list the authors in alphabetical order within the same parentheses, and separate their names with semicolons. If the author's work is in still press (i.e. accepted by journal but not yet identified with the volume and issue of publication), write "in press" to replace the year of publication:

(Baurn & Benson, in press; Brydges & Smith, 2010; Wong, 1997; Zunderland & Li, 2007)

Harvard: Citations - Same Author for Different Source, Different Years

If you are citing several representative sources for a key point that are written by the same author in different years, you only need to show the author's last name once, and then list the year of publication for his/her additional works. Show the earliest work first. Separate them with comma and not semicolons:

(Wong, 2001, 2005, 2009)

Harvard: Citations - Same Author for Different Source, Same Year

If you are citing several representative sources for a key point that are written by the same author in the same year, you only need to show the author's last name once, and then add suffixes "a", "b", and "c"…etc after the year of publication to distinguish these references. Separate them with comma and not semicolons:

(Wong, 2009a, 2009b)

Harvard: Citations - Secondary Source

During your literature review, you may come across an article that includes a citation of another article that you cannot locate. It may be out-of-print, written in another language, or simply not available through the regular library access. Without reading the original article yourself, there is a risk to cite that source because you did not know about the context of the original paper. Having said that, if you strongly believe that you want to make reference to these materials, here's how you should do it:

In other words, you cite the primary/original source in the text, and then list the secondary source in the references section.

Let's say Smith published an article in 1969 and it is subsequently cited in Wong's article in 2010. Assuming you did not read Smith's original work, you should:

1. In the text, write…according to Smith (1969) as cited in Wong (2010)

2. In the references section, list Wong's paper.

Harvard: Citations - Multimedia works

If it's a CD-ROM, use the title of the CD-ROM as the author. If it is a video tape or DVD, use the series title as the author.

Examples:

(Anatomy of Human Beings - Version 5.0, 2010)

Harvard: References - Book - One Author

Author's last name, first initial. (Year of publication) *Title of book in italic type*. Place of publication, Publisher.

If the author's first name is hyphenated (e.g. Kwong-Kay Wong), keep the hyphen and include a period after each initial.

Example:

Wong, K.-K. (2010) *The Academic Writing Guide*. New York, NY, Another University Press.

Harvard: References - Book - Same Author, Different Years

If the same author has written articles in different years, list them by year of publication with the earliest first.

Example:

Smith, D. (2002) *Hypotheses and facts*. New York, NY, Another University Press.

Smith, D. (2010) *Theory on children behavior*. New York, NY, Another University Press.

Similar to citation, use suffixes "a", "b", "c", "d"…etc to distinguish one book from another.

Example:

Smith, D. (2010a) *Hypotheses and facts*. New York, NY, Another University Press.

Smith, D. (2010b) *Theory on children behavior*. New York, NY, Another University Press.

Author's last name, first initial & second author last name, first initial (Year) *Title of book*. Place of publication, Publisher.

Example:

Smith, G. & Kim, M. (2010) *Of course you're happy: a guide to deal with emotional challenges* (Rev. ed.). Toronto, ON, Another University Press.

Please note that one-author entries precede multiple-author entries, even if the multiple-author entries were published earlier:

Example:

Smith, D. (2010) *Hypotheses and facts*. New York, NY, Another University Press.

Smith, D. & Thomson, J. (1997) *Guide to Marketing*. New York, NY, Another University Press.

Harvard: References - Book - Organizational/Group Author

Group author. (Year). *Title of book*. Place of publication, Publisher.

Example:

American Children Association. (2010) *Children violence in America*. New York, NY, Another University Press.

If a Digital Object Identifier (DOI) is available with the book, please print it at the end, right after the publisher.

Example:

American Children Association. (2009) *Children violence in America*. New York, NY, Another University Press. doi:10/1013/30422-000

Harvard: References - Book - No Author

Anon (Year) *Title of book*. Place of publication, Publisher.

Note: "Anon" means anonymous and this is suggested in the Imperial College version of the Harvard styles. In other Harvard versions, you are asked to just use the book title as author name instead.

Example:

Anon (2010) *Example of Book Title*. New York, Academic Press.

Harvard: References - Book - No Authors, Only Editors

Editor last name, first initial. (ed.). (Year) *Title of book*. Place of publication, Publisher.

Example:

Smith, P. & Wong, K. (eds.). (2010) *Perspectives on children development*. Toronto, ON, Canadian University Press.

Harvard: References - Book - Edition Other Than the First

Author last name, first initial. (Year) *Title of book.* (Edition, if not the first edition). Place of publication, Publisher.

Example:

Smith, J. (2010) *Field guide to marketing.* (2nd ed.). Toronto, ON, Canadian University Press.

Note: if the book is in its first edition, there is no need to show it.

Harvard: References - Book - Chapter or Article in an Edited Book

Author's last name, first initial. (Year) Title of Article. In: Editor's last name and first initial (ed.) *Title of book.* Volume or edition number. Place of publication, Publisher. page numbers.

Note: Some Harvard styles would need you to print the editor's first name initial and then his/her last name, such as "In: J. Smith" instead of "In: Smith, J."

Example:

Smith, J. (2010) The Issue of Plagiarism. In: Kim, S. (ed.), *Guide To Good Academic Writing*, Vol. 1, Toronto, ON, Canadian University Press. pp.207-208.

Harvard: References - Book - Translated from Other Language

Author's last name, first initial. (Year) *Book Title.* Trans. Last name of translator, first initial of translator. Other identifiers such as series, volume, or edition. Place of publication, Publisher.

Example:

Lee, T. (2010) *Learning Trends.* Trans. Smith, J. Vol. 1, Toronto, ON, Another University Press.

Harvard: References - Conference Proceedings (Officially Published)

Author's last name, first initial. (Year) Title of paper. In: Editor's last name, first initial (ed.) *Title of Conference Proceedings*. Place of Publication, Publisher, page range.

Example:

Smith, J. (2010) Impact of the e-learning platform on distance learner. In: Wong, S (ed.) *International Council for Distance Education Conference 2010*. Toronto, ON, Canadian University Press, pp. 179-185.

Harvard: References - Conference Presentations (Not Officially Published)

Author's last name, first initial. (Year) *Title of paper*. Paper presented at Title of Conference, Location.

Example:

Smith, J. R. (2010) *Working with visually-challenged students: An integrated theoretical model*. Paper presented at the Symposium of the Canadian Education Association World Conference, Toronto, ON.

Harvard: References - Data Set

Name of Data Set Provider. (Year of Publication) *Name of Data Set* [Online]. Available from URL of the Data Set. [Date of Access].

Example:

Statistics Canada. (2010) *CENSUS 2006 Employment Report* [Online]. Available from http://www.statscan.gc.ca/datasets/1234567.html/ [Accessed 3rd Aug, 2010].

Note: if you cannot locate the year of publication, write the abbreviation (n.d.) for no date.

Example:

Statistics Canada. (n.d.) *CENSUS 2006 Employment Report* [Online]. Available from http://www.statscan.gc.ca/datasets/1234567.html/ [Accessed 3rd Aug, 2010].

Harvard: References - Dissertations and Theses - from ERIC Database

ERIC stands for the Educational Resources Information Center in the USA. If the dissertation is retrieved from its database, the reference format will look like:

Author last name, first initial. (Year) *Title of dissertation*. PhD thesis. Imperial College London. Retrieved from ERIC database. (ED code)

Example:

Smith, C. A. (2007) *Studying from remote provinces in Canada: A cross-sectional study*. PhD thesis. Retrieved from ERIC database. (ED4123967)

Harvard: References - Dissertations and Theses - from ProQuest

Author's last name, first initial. (Year) *Title of dissertation*. PhD thesis. Name of University. Available from Database Name. (Dissertation identification code)

Example:

Smith, C. A. (2007) *Studying from remote provinces in Canada: A cross-sectional study*. PhD thesis. University of Toronto. Available from ProQuest Dissertations and Theses database. (UMI No. 4123967)

Harvard: References - Dissertations and Theses - from Institutional Database

Author's last name, first initial. (Year) *Title of dissertation*. PhD thesis. Name of University. Retrieved from URL of database.

Example:

Smith, J. (2010) *Model for Strategic Marketing in the Banking Sector*. PhD thesis. University of Toronto. Retrieved from http://www.utoronto.ca/etd/phd12345.html

Harvard: References - Encyclopedia or Dictionary (Online)

Author's last name, first initial. (n.d. which stands for no date). Entry heading. In *Title of encyclopedia* (volume number and then page number, if applicable. Otherwise, use edition information). Retrieved from URL

Example:

Smith, C. (n.d.). Shopaholic syndrome. In *Canadian Women Encyclopedia* (Fall 2010 ed.). Retrieved from http://www.utoronto.ca/entries12346

Note: if you cannot locate the author's name, place the book title in the author's position.

Harvard: References - Encyclopedia or Dictionary (Print)

Author's last name, first initial. (Year) Entry heading. In *Title of encyclopedia* (volume number and then page number, if applicable). Place of publication, Publisher.

Example:

Smith, J. (2010) Social Networking. In *New Canadian dictionary* (vol.26: pp.123-124). Toronto, ON, Another University Press.

Note: if you cannot locate the author's name, place the book title in the author's position.

Harvard: References - Google Books (Online)

Author last name, first initial. (Year) *Title of work*. [Online] Place of publication: Publisher. Retrieved from URL (Access date)

Example:

Smith, J. (2010) *International Marketing*. [Online] New York, NY, Another University Press. Retrieved from http://books.google.com/books12345.html (Accessed 18th May 2010)

Harvard: References - Interview or Personal Communications

Name of person interviewed. Interviewed by: Name of interviewer. (Date of interview)

Example:

Smith, J. Interviewed by Susan, M. (4th May 2009).

Harvard: References - Journal Article with DOI assigned.

Author's last name, first initial. (Year) Title of article. *Title of journal*. [Online] Volume number (issue number), page numbers. DOI information. [Access date].

Example:

Smith, J. (2010) Brand Extension Strategy for Japanese Brands. *Journal of International Marketing*. [Online] 32(2), 50-52. doi:20.1022/0202-1232.77.4.321 [Accessed 2 Jan 2010].

Harvard: References - Journal Article - Retrieved from an Online Subscription Database

Author's last name, first initial. (Year) Title of article. *Title of journal.* [Online] Volume number(issue number), page numbers. Retrieved from URL of the article. [Access date].

Example:

Smith, T.-J., Jr. (2010) Information literacy for homeschoolers. *International Journal of Library Management.* [Online] 32(4), pp. 50-52. Retrieved from http://www.library.org/article12345.html [Accessed 4 Feb 2010].

If the journal has ceased to exist and/or there's no home page for the journal, use the name of database instead.

Example:

Smith, B. (1923) The experience of a junior high principal. *Journal of School Management.* [Online] 3(7). Retrieved from JSTOR database. [Accessed 4 Feb 2010].

Harvard: References - Journal Article - (Printed Version)

Author last name, first initial & second author's last name and first initial. (Year) Title of article. *Title of journal.* Volume number(month of publication), page number.

Example:

Smith, J. & Susan, M. (2010) Branding strategies for Canadian firms. *International Journal of Marketing*, 24(3), pp. 14-20.

Harvard: References - Magazine - No Author

Magazine Name (Publication date) Article Name. Vol (issue), page range.

Example:

Canadian Financial Magazine (5 Mar 2010) All You Need to Know About RRSP and RESP. 30(2), pp. 5-7.

Harvard: References - Magazine - One Author

Author's last name, first initial. (Publication date) Article Name. *Magazine Name*, vol (issue), page range.

Example:

Smith, J.R. (10 July 2010) Marketing in the 21st Century. *Canadian Business Magazine*, 190 (2), pp. 63-67.

Harvard: References - Newspaper - Online

Author's last name, first initial. (Day, month and year of publication). Article Name. *Newspaper Name* [Online] page number. Available from: URL [Date of access].

Example:

Smith, T. S. (15 February 2010) The 911 Incident Re-Visited. *New York Times*. [Online] Available from: http://www.nytimes. com/2010/23e1341f5.html. [Accessed 2nd July 2010].

Note: If the article has no author, use the newspaper name as author's.

Harvard: References - Newspaper - Print

Author's last name, first initial. (Day, month and year of publication) Article Name. *Newspaper Name*, page numbers.

Example:

Smith, J. (30 March 2010) Do we need the long Census form?. *The Globe and Mail.* p.B2.

Harvard: References - Online Communities (Blogs, Forums, Newsgroups, Social Networking Sites)

Author's last name, first initial. (year of publication). Title of post. Message type. [Online]. Available from: URL [Access date].

Example:

Smith, J. F. (2010) Problems of Facebook [Online]. Available from http://groups.google.com/group/facebook/12345.html/ [Accessed 18th June 2010]

Harvard: References - Recordings (DVDs, CDs, Tape)

Title (Year of production) [media type] Place of production or origin. Name of production company/maker.

Examples:

The mummy (2004) [DVD]. New York, NY, MCA Universal Home Video.

The Twin Tower Story (2010) [DVD]. Toronto, ON, Universal ABC Video.

Harvard: References - Specialized Software with Limited Distribution

Author's last name, first initial. (Year of publication). *Title of software or computer program* (Version number) [Format type]. Place of publication, Name of publisher. Available from: URL (if online)

Example:

Ringle, C., Wende, S. & Will A. (2005). *SmartPLS 2.0* (beta) [Software] Hamburg, Germany, University of Hamburg. Available from http://www.smartpls.de.

P.S.: if you cannot identify the name of the author or editor, use the corporation/organization's name in the author's place.

Harvard: References - Technical and Research Reports (Online)

Author's last name, first initial. (Year of publication). *Title of publication*. Organization name. Report number: Available from: URL. [Access date]

Example:

Smith, F. D., Kim, R., & Wong, A. (2010) *Populations of the Caribbean, 2009*. Statistic Bureau of the Caribbean. Report No. 1234567: Available from http://www.statisticcaribbean.org/pubs2009/2009RL1234567.pdf [Accessed 3 May 2010]

If the author is unknown, treat the government department or agency as the group author. If the report only has an editor but not an author, always put (ed.) after the name.

Harvard: References - Unpublished Academic Paper Retrieved Online

Author's last name, first initial. (Year or publication or n.d. for no date) *Title of article*. Unpublished thesis. Location, name of institution, program and/or department. Available from: URL. [Access date].

Example:

Smith, J. C. (n.d.) *Comparisons of school performance between boys and girls in the 12-20 age group*. Unpublished thesis. Toronto, University of Toronto, Programs for Children Education, Faculty of Arts and Science,

Available from http://www.utoronto.ca/phd /phd/online_documents. htm/ [Accessed 4 July 2010].

Harvard: References - Web Article without Author

Name of Organization. (Year of publication, or n.d. for no date). *Title of the web article*. [Online]. Available from: URL. [Date of access]

Example:

University of Toronto (2010). *President's Opinion on Academic Freedom*. [Online]. Available from: http://www.utoronto.ca/abcde1234.html. [Accessed 5 Jan 2010].

Harvard: References - Web Article with Author

Author last name, first initial. (Year of publication) *Title of web article*. [Online] Available from: URL. [Date of Access].

Example:

Smith, T. (2010, May 2) *What has to be changed at Facebook?* Available from http://www.salon.com/2010/05/02/facebook/index.html. [Accessed 5 Aug 2010].

Harvard: References - YouTube Video

Author last name, first initial. (year) 'File Name' [Video file]. Available from: URL. [Access date]

Example:

Smith, J. A. (2010). 'The Unboxing of my Apple iPad' [Video file]. Available from http://www.YouTube.com/group/watch?v=TGJ7h43nsu_ Id. [Accessed 9 June 2010].

Note: The title of the video is not italicized.

EPILOGUE

I hope you have enjoyed reading this book and found it useful in your study.

By now, you should have invested some valuable time going through the various writing examples. The good students will turn theories into action and start using proper citing and referencing styles in their next paper assignment. The bad ones will say "forget it, that's just too difficult!" and get back to their comfort zone to repeat the bad writing behavior. My advice? Start to write properly now, and don't wait till next class, next semester, or next year.

To those who are browsing this book right now at Chapters/Indigo, just pay for it and evaluate the book leisurely at home for 2 weeks. Don't stand in the aisle for the whole afternoon! Remember to keep your original receipt if you intend to get a full refund at the bookstore later.

If you have purchased this book as part of Dr. Wong's course, thank you. I hope this little book can help you write better papers to earn higher grades.

If you have just downloaded this book from those illegal websites and would like to keep it on your computer for future reference, you have three options:

1. Go to iUniverse's official web site to purchase a legitimate electronic copy. I have intentionally made the ebook version affordable (about US$10) so that my students can enjoy it without costing them an arm and a leg. Helping you to understand the concept of intellectual properties is one of my teaching objectives.

2. Make a donation to your local charity or become a volunteer. I really mean it. If you absolutely don't want to pay the publisher for whatever reasons, please at least make a difference to help other people in your community.

3. Do nothing, if you think stealing is the right thing to do.

Have a great day and thanks for taking time to read my work.

Cheers,

Ken

Bibliography

American Psychological Association. (2010). *Publication Manual of the American Psychological Association.* (6th ed.) Washington, DC: American Psychological Association.

Colomb, G. (2010). Understanding Plagiarism and Paraphrasing: A University of Virginia Honor Committee Supplement. Charlottesville, VA: University of Virginia. Retrieved from http://www.virginia.edu/honor/documents/ PlagiarismSupplementFINAL.pdf

Cronje, M, Murdoch, N. & Smit, R. (ed.) (2008). *Reference Techniques: Harvard methods and APA style.* (2nd ed.). Auckland Park, South Africa: University of Johannesburg. Retrieved from http://www.uj.ac.za/EN/Library/Documents/REFERENCE%20 TECHNIQUES%202008%20Harvard%20Method%20and%20 APA%20Style.pdf

Harvard Business School. (2009). *Citation Guide 2009-10 Academic Year.* Boston, MA: Harvard Business School. Retrieved from http://www.library.hbs.edu/guides/citationguide.pdf

Harvard Citation Style. (2010). *LibGuides Home.* Perth, Australia: The University of Western Australia. Retrieved from http:// libguides.library.uwa.edu.au/harvard

Harvard Referencing Guide. (2010). *the Library - Subjects & support.* London, UK: Imperial College London. Retrieved from http://www3.imperial.ac.uk/library/subjectsandsupport/ referencemanagement/harvard

How to... use the Harvard reference system. (2010). *How To Guides.* Bingley, UK: Emerald Group Publishing Limited. Retrieved from http://www.emeraldinsight.com/authors/guides/write/harvard.htm?part=1

Matto, M. (2009). *Faculty Tips on Preventing Plagiarism*. Garden City, NY: Adelphi University. Retrieved from http://academics.adelphi.edu/academicintegrity/pdfs/prevent_plagiarism.pdf

The Honor Committee (2010). Fraud and the Honor System. *What is Academic Fraud?* . Charlottesville, VA: University of Virginia. Retrieved from http://www.virginia.edu/honor/fraud.html

The University of Chicago Press. (2010). *The Chicago Manual of Style*. (16th ed.). Chicago, IL: The University of Chicago Press.